Sixty-Five Years Till Now

ENGAGE BOOKS

WWW.ENGAGEBOOKS.CA

Victoria Roscoe Hazlehurst © 2010

Edited by A. R. Roumanis

Cover photo by Victoria Roscoe Hazlehurst © 2010

Typeset by A.R. Roumanis
Text set in 10.7/13 Aldus
Chapter headings set in 10/20 Palatino

Hazlehurst, Victoria Roscoe, 1945 –

ISBN: 978-1-926606-37-8

Note on the author: Victoria Roscoe-Roumanis has expressed that she would go by the pen name Victoria R. Hazlehurst, should she ever publish a book. Hazlehurst is her maiden name.

Editors note: The first edition was compiled from nearly two hundred hand written poems, without guidance from the author on areas that could have been interpreted differently than what the author originally intended. Also, the author had not read through the typeset material. This revised first edition has been edited by the author, and changed to the author's satisfaction. Most notably, seven new poems were added on pages 60, 62, 106, 135, 142 & 175. Prior to this revised edition, 57 copies were printed.

Engage Books
PO Box 4608
Main Station Terminal
349 West Georgia Street
Vancouver, BC
V6B 4A1
Canada

Sixty-Five Years Till Now

Victoria R. Hazlehurst

*"As my feet met the pebbles, it felt as
if the earth was crumbling beneath me."*
Victoria R. Hazlehurst – 20th September 2005

ENGAGE BOOKS / VANCOUVER

Contents

Introduction

I always wondered about those times that my Mom was staring off into the distance. Sitting still while she gazed out the window at the crisp water of Sproat Lake, the power of Battleship Island, and snow peaked Mount Klitsa. Just sitting, and to my young ears, doing nothing.

When I was young, my brothers and I were always busy doing things that little boys do. Swimming in the lake, trekking through the forest, and building tree forts. We were always moving, running, fighting. And we used soccer, rugby and wrestling as an outlet for this raw energy.

Through all of this, how did my Mom keep still. The idea of sitting still was unfathomable to our young minds, starving for new experiences. When I got older I realized that she was very busy reliving her life in her memories. But it wasn't until I had read through my Mom's poems that I developed a new appreciation for this understanding. When she was sitting still she was stuffing her pockets with candies from her Grandmother's store, riding her horse Jupiter on the English countryside, and partying with friends in London.

Mom has had so many wonderful memories throughout her life, and she found comfort and peace in writing them onto the page. Her poems of natural settings portray an amazing view of the world through her eyes. Many of her poems are filled with twists and turns that would make Lewis Carroll proud, love that will touch your soul, and a fear that would make Mary Shelley tremble. She has written about our family with love and affection, and looks back on her youth with a fondness for memories that will always stay with her.

It is with pride that I am able to present this book to my mom as a surprise for her sixty-fifth birthday. Having scanned these poems from various handwritten notebooks on the ruse that they would be lost if there was a fire, encouraging my mom that she should type them out and send them to a publisher, and explaining to her the sad truth that a poetry book which sells 400 copies is considered a success in Canada, I know that she will be surprised. My Mom has done so much for me, and I can't wait for when she sees the book for the first time at her surprise book launch among family and friends.

Mom and I have shared so many wonderful moments. Finding a beach to explore on a hot summers day, playing badminton with our dog Paris searching for tennis balls, and picking dandelions in the garden. Sitting still, I will always look back on those fond memories with Mom and remember.

Alexandros R. Roumanis
April 2010

Mother Nature

Rainfall

Mountains catch raindrops with open arms
The first to feel their soft refreshing touch
The high elevation cannot contain their number
Droplets huddle together forming silver ribbons
Flowing down from peaks as if blown by the wind

The speed of their descent increases
Torrents of water flow until at the foot
Where the incline is more gentle
The frantic rush is subdued
Tired droplets join those that went before
Drifting along elegantly to catch the ocean's tide

The Raging Bull

The wind was in a playful mood last night
Playful as a young bull wanting to show his strength
His strength was powerful

Listening to him blow
One could almost feel the tree roots being drawn out of the ground
Hear their limbs being torn and tossed like chaff from a threshing floor

His presence caused me to feel powerless against him
No delete bar to push
Powerless against the force of nature

This was just a young wind,
Imagine being in the eye of a hurricane,
Blown like an autumn leaf in any direction he chooses

Similarly, the rain tumbles from the sky
Like a gigantic waterfall washing the whole world clean
At least our corner of it

Snowdrop

You greet us in winter
Matching the snow
Tiny, delicate blossom
Courage and strength bestow
Promise of spring
Sets hearts aglow

Bear in Moonshine

Stars swimming in the moonshine
Like orange and yellow sprinkles
On chocolate cake
Until disturbed by the wildlife
A bear hunting to fill his round tummy before dawn
Enjoying throwing himself deep
Like a sack of rock-hard potatoes
Unashamedly disturbing the quiet of majestic forest

Pasture

Behind the blackberries in the lane
The herd gathers in the green field
Closely cutting blades
Breathing silence
Wide nostrils exhale breath
Scents of summer pasture
Carried on evening breeze

White on White

Silently snowflakes fall
Like feathers from a tree
Floating as the wind blows
Finding an earthly resting place
Gently filling every crevice
Until the earth with all its clutter
Becomes white on white

Earth

It's an earthly thing
Just can't explain
Basic – Down to Earth good
That feeds the soul

Closure on a Warm September Evening

Caught my eye as I glanced out the window
The sky wearing a coat of radical red
Changing each second in a glorious light show
With a backdrop of blue and silver sky
Drops of water coloured by the mighty palate
Reflected on the gentle ripples of the lake

Sun slides down to rest
Behind Mt. Klitsa's black velvet silhouette
Silver blue sky set ablaze
With tongues of brilliant red and burnt orange
Reflecting out across the lake

Dancing on the ripples
Until the dock under my feet breaks their path
Now it's here, now it's gone
Changing as fast as the doused flames of a camp fire
In an instant, Darkness envelops the silver grey water

Fireflies in Wood

Sky black as the coat of the lucky cat
Speckled by sparks of light
As if spewed from a Roman candle
Tumbling down to engulf the earth
Look out it's coming at you

Shimmering Waves

Home with Alexis
Down to the beach
Swimming in the shimmering
Silver speckled clear water
All the stress of the day
Carried away on the quiet waves
Held weightless
Breathing in the beauty
Of this wonderful corner
Of the world I live in

The Eerie Cove

The silhouette of the young beech trees on the top of the cliff
Gave a photographic image of anorexic sticks,
Lost for words in the bleakness of this wind swept, eerie cove

Peak About

The sun broke through the wild tones of grey in the sky
Two regal trees robed in the heart of winter live their bleakness
They frame the view of the Somas River
Looking out through café windows
In the cozy warmth with my friend
The sun going down
The moon rising as I walked home
Playing peak about through winters noble trees

Wild Pacific Trail

The trail was tame
It was the Pacific that was wild
Power from the depths
Pushed up, giant furrows of raging sea
Breaking open on rocky black teeth

Spraying white tassels into the air
Like spirited white horses running wild
Tossing their manes
To the sound of thundering hooves
Onlookers, in awe keep their distance
Lest they be trampled by the ocean's force

Star Fly

Star fly
Far across black
Velvety soft and dark
Line of brightness where do you go
So fast

Lonely Tranquility

"You do not have to sit outside in the dark. If, however, you want to look at the stars you will find the darkness necessary."
– Annie Dylard

On a night lit by stars
She wound her way down to the beech
Accompanied by just the faintest sound of water movement
As it kissed the stony shore

Lying on the dock
Watching the sky move around her
A star shoots – a satellite flicks its way through the blackness
She hears the hum of a jet on its flight path
High, high above

Lowering her eyes she looks out across the water
The dark silhouette of the mountains
Standing like powerful sentries
On guard for this fragile lake
Which shimmers innocently in the moon glow

The air suddenly cools
She feels the chill and returns to the warmth of her cabin
Taking with her the image of lonely tranquility

Summer's Ending

Crickets sounding
Like a squeaky mill wheel
Spinning to make time

Boat racing – engine groans
Like a cat's purr
Disturbing the tranquil lake

Sounds of imagined silence
Dogs barking, water lapping
Birds singing, busy crickets

Bright setting sun
Settles on bare branches
Like crystalline snow in winter

Wild blue asters poke through stones
Ragged petals dancing
In the soft breeze

The clouds silver lining
Squishes out from darkened pillows
Like cream from a chocolate éclair

Lake, do you comfort me?
With ripples lapping the shore
I remember the waters of the cradling womb

Does the flow of my blood sense security?
Responding to your movement
Recalling a safer time

Don't leave sun, everything changes
Colour drained, like a sepia photo
Warmth disappears, like doused embers
Summer is fading away

Autumn Day

Dimpled water, black and silver
Silently moving
As the last rays of sun glimmer
Before taking its leave behind the mountain
To an orchestra of crickets
Singing in defiance of the autumn day
Eagle calls
Fish jump
Knowing there is no one here to catch them
They forget about the eagles
Crickets sound like a phone left off the hook
Or the constant warning of the car door left open

It should be quiet here
In vision rippled steel water
Which runs to the foot of slate grey mountains
Like cardboard cut-outs against a grey sky
Yet sound all around
Crickets monotonous chirps
Fish making splashes
Birds settling after the day
A bee flying by
He should be gone in this season
All the sounds of the carpenters tools
Building the new home on the corner
The sound of chill
Calling me indoors

Temporary Peace

Windows opening onto the light
Channeling vision to the lakes view
A wooden dock
A row boat
Framed by an all encompassing mist
A backdrop to feelings
Eyes weightless as they float over the beauty
Cushioning heavy thoughts which are drawn out into light
Forgetting the imbalance of unknown decisions

Silver Circles on the Lake Today

Looking down at the lake from my window
I see there are circles on the lake today
Beautiful, silver, concentric circles
Flowing out until they dissipate

The lakes surface, the artists canvas,
Is suddenly bare again
I wait several minutes for the creative ones to reappear
My patience is rewarded as the little swimmers bob up
Through the water's ripples
They take air – then dive and dimple the water again
Painting shimmering, glimmering circles
Circles of learning and fun
Circles of spring activity

The light and wind have changed
The water's surface is choppy now
I see the mother diving with her seven little ducklings,
There are no silver circles to draw my eye
As they perfect their skilful maneuvers
Only little brown feathered bundles
Bobbing on toned grey water

Golden Oak

Majestic and mighty stands the oak
Self confident in its strength
Limbs reaching out to touch the sky
Giving thanks for great beauty

Hundreds of years have passed
As the oaks stand on guard
Like sentinels over green hill and vale
Bare in winter splendour

Dark arms sway in the wind
Changing raiment to
Crisp, spring green foliage
Light and airy

Summer maturity shading the lanes
Then Autumn couture drapes the limbs
In all its royal, golden pageantry

Sun

She is dazzled with sun light
As it plays hide and seek
With clouds black and heavy
Dropping out of sight then
Kicking up a fire water display of colour
"Coming, ready or not"

Time running out
No longer able to bounce back
To rekindle the darkening sky
Game lost to the mountains
Which take on the duty of sentries
Towering above the dark velvet water
Keeping guard until the dawn of a new day

Unwinding

Heaven wore her blue coat in the morning
The waters reflected their joy in her beauty
Infinite mountains in their green raiments
Reach up to touch the blue
Crystal air gently embraced the earth
Crows made up a percussion
Expectant of tasty bounty

Sea plane revs its engine
Disturbing the silence
Yet rewarding the passengers
With a view too awe inspiring to fully grasp
The remote Indian village quickly found
Unwinding life's trials for the travellers

Bernard was waiting on the dock
With dogs and wheelbarrow
To porter luggage to the lodge
Two thankful spirits
Raised their thanks to Him
For this privilege and blessing
For eyes to see
For ears to hear
Emotions to feel the radiance

A Boardwalk Hour

Star from the East
A lighthouse beacon
Guiding the night into day
The sun climbed over the ebony mountains
Standing on guard for this secluded cove
And the lodge in a remote Indian village

Heaven has come to Earth here
Thanks be to God
Bernard transports the two across the calm inlet
To connect to the trail of the hot springs
When it was thought all the beauty had been seen
Eyes beheld a magnificence unimaginable

The rainforests cathedral entrance rose above them
Displaying centuries of growth
Twisted and turning roots anchored their load
Meeting delicate leaves of ground cover

The boardwalk inspiring in itself
With the thoughts of its travellers
Carved for eternity
Beneath our feet

After a boardwalk hour
Rays of sun lit up the rising steam of the hot springs
A theatrical entrance to the pools
Cocooned in the rocks at maximum heat
Steaming falls showering over responsive flesh

If life should cease today
The last day of summer
In the company of my dearest friend
It would be an amazingly peaceful end

Fun with Mum

Rain-race

Challenging the drops to run down the pain
Slowly at first until several gathered together
Then it was a race to the line
Thousands ran the race
Eager to show their skill
Unaware of their fate
Until they drowned in the puddle on the sill

Love of a Steam Train

I hear his powerful rumble in the distance
And my heart goes out to meet him
He is easy to spot veiled in a wreath of white steam
Metal wheels and track set a rhythm that echoes in my soul
His proud whistle signals warning and greeting

Comfort and security build
A loved one returning
Briefly enfolding me in his strong arms
Then reluctantly letting go
Leaving me to watch until the horizon is free of his silhouette
His passing stirs deep emotions

It seems as if he calls
"Come with me, we'll travel together,
"Come with me, we'll have fun together,
"Come with me, I'll love you forever!"

Earthlings

Earthen
Earth first
No Earthly reason
What on Earth
Peace on Earth
Earthlings

Mice on Treadmills

Imagine the mouse in his cage
Treading the wheel
Running as if the Farmer's wife were after him
Certain he will get away but where to
Bars with no opening
Stationary treadmills enclosed by gym walls
Men and women running
Mile after mile
Eyes set on

Toonie Toonie

Now there's a name for you
Great intro for a piano tuner
Or a quiz game
How about a tuny fish anniversary
Tiny, tiny tuna,

Just like Tim
Remember him
Down on a house boat
Singing a seafaring toon

The streets of London Town sang his toon
Dan on the dock with his guitar
Knew all the toonie's he did
Now it's time to toon out

Catapult

Smooth Stone
Right dimension
Ready set aim and fire
Hit the can is my intention

Rainwood Writers

Come sit at our ping-pong table
And we'll write you a line
It doesn't matter if you're able
Our words will make you shine
Rainwood writers will send you a cable
And we'll all just get along fine

Kite on a String

Each day tells its own tale
One beat at a time
Pulsating along our winding paths
There are no certainties
Always the unexpected

Blow for me wind
Brush your cool on my cheeks
Ruffle my hair
Fill me with your breath
Carry me to heights never imagined
Shelter me in the crevice of freedom
Lay down beside me with your warmth
Carry my cares

Soon reality,
Like a kite at the end of a string
Controlling
Only going so far
Reigning back
Capturing the body
Coming down with a thud
On the earth

Drinking Butter Tea

Something is frightfully wrong
The butter is in the T-pot
Tea is on the bread
What time is it?
Time for tea said the rabbit

Butter in the hat
That's *mad*
Must be something to do with the Dormouse
Table mouse – sitting on the T-pot
Tea – Hot runny – buttercup yellow
Black speckled bread
"Would you like to drink butter-tea my dear" enquired the hatter
"No thank you," said Alice, "I haven't got 10/6"
I need to follow the white rabbit

The Debt Clock

It's eight-fifteen and the national debt passes 7 trillion US dollars
The clock strikes nine
They are out on a line
And Bush got mangled up in the machinery

The Paths of Pilgrims

In a monastery garden
The leaves, seeds and flowers fall
Blown to the ground by warm dessert breeze
In the calm of the morning

Two black robed monks report for duty
Armed with the power to disturb the silence
The demon machine revs and hums,

A knife to the ears
Blowing fallen leaves
From the path of pilgrims
Please God grant silence or refuge

My Damn Cell Phone Costs too Much

There's the call waiting, the voice mail
Calls to children away – $109 for August
Then there's my pager – always at my side
There's no escape – one day I might take rest

The cell phone – a must to call back to work
Within the allotted 5 minutes to grasp a work day
What use is it – always writes me a messages saying
No Service Area – almost everywhere in town

Back to the good old call box
Well it's cheaper, only a quarter
Compared to .33 cents a minute
It seems impossible to disconnect
If I had to chose between e-mail and the phone
The damn phone takes the vote

The Triangle

There are always two sides to every story
However, when there are three
The fat is really in the fire,
There has to be smoke

Yet the stitch in time never saves nine
When the bird in the bush takes flight
Out of sight of the mind
We roll the stone without moss
Until all the glass houses shatter

Blowing Steam

In Steamers, looked up to see the steam train,
Steam, letting go of pressure,
Blowing steam, steam to fill paragraphs

Throw the tension onto the soft bed of steam
Cushioning each movement,
At first letting the body fall softly until limbs release
I float effortlessly cocooned in the air of release

Take my thoughts down the track with the quenching rhythm,
Out to the retreats of the mind
The railway banks with the yellow of primroses,
The velvet of violets

Sitting, watching the steam ooze out of the tunnel
As the black iron machine pokes his head through
A friendly toot of his whistle as he sees me there
Air surrounding me,
Refreshing the memories of youth

The Snail & the Tortoise

23 days to the bottom of the hill
Said the snail to the tortoise,
You're talking out of your shell

Shells don't roll,
Rolling moss lines the dips and the curves
The grass is greener down below

Green grow the rushes oh
Rushes bend with the speed of the wind
Speed to the bottom, to free the race

The Rattle of Teacups

A comforting sound
Signals a time to pause,
A visit with a friend,
Tables on the sidewalk
Beckoning social interaction

The rattling of teacups
A musical sound rallying
Tea with grandmother under the lilac trees
The sound of teacups in the kitchen early in the morning
Encouraging the greeting of day

Meeting at Steamers with good friends,
On a warm summers day,
Or a cold, windy inlet day
Rattling teacups have power to calm cares away

Why Didn't Adam & Eve have Children in Paradise

When Eve gave the apple to Adam,
He was tempted to dig in his teeth and bite
When God reminded him of his sin
He threw the apple back to Eve

She did not like the look on his face
And began to race until she was outside Eden
The grass was too long
She tumbled and fell
Young Adam fell close on her heals

David's Sling

The runway vibrated
While the jet's engines whirled
As if they were about to explode
Just as it seemed the cement and my ears,
Could not take the noise and vibration any longer
The plane shot forward,
Like a stone from David's sling,
Hurtling off down the runway
Until effortlessly it took to the air,
Destiny infinity

Snowbirds

Live to fly
Playing with air
Daring – gravity
Flying to dive

Mars Water Bombers

Sounds of Mars bomber engines
Resonate and bounce
From mountain to mountain around the lake
Like giant bees on a mission
Scooping up water to fill the hold

Then forward throttle
Lifting heavy red wings skyward
Barely clearing surrounding forest
Silence, quickly broken moments later
By the sound of these super birds

Repeating its fire drill
Taking off to douse the fire
Somewhere not too far off
Again and again
These magnificent fire fighting birds take our attention

On the last flyby the hatches open
And the cargo is dropped over Dog Mountain
Signifying a job well done
Fire must be out
This load not required
Our security team head back to base
One more success story to tell

The Light Bulb

A child's eyes strained upwards
Discerning movements in the luminous globe
He seemed to be busy up there
At times with a companion

It appeared to her eye as if he was sometimes in a sealed capsule
A trucker's cabin
Squinting eyes try to penetrate the mysterious glass sphere
Is he trying to get out?

Hang Tight

Boiling over
Relief is found in the whirling fan blades
Spinning – forcing the air
Cooling, extinguishing the rage of the furness
Resembling life's furness
Escape is only a brief movement
A step to the side
Throws one back into the fire of battle

And we battle,
We believe we have it tamed
Really think we have won
Then in an instant the heat is turned on
As we grasp the arms of the propeller
And just pray we don't fall
Hang tight

To Find the Unicorn King

You just started streaming – sorry to be late
I obviously missed the evenings preamble
The banter, and exchange which weaves us together
Woven like reads to form a strong retainer to hold our thoughts,

Wisdom and creative rhymes
Sharing, testing the water
Pens running along the page
Like a pea green boat on the turn of the tide

Snow owl, no pussy cat, only a ring of bright water
Let's sail away for a year and a day
Would the sea release its sunlit golden ring
If we gave it a shilling
The mermaid to ride away
Carried over the waves by the Unicorn King

King of the sea horses
Effortlessly gliding
Springing on his haunches over the glistening silver waves
Off through the sunlight
The moons shadows
Till that far off land of heaven brings peace and rest

What is Rest at Sixty-Five

Words
Stars, trees, shopping, money, rush, stress
Stress, now there is my word for the day
Pick me up, take me away, land me in an oasis,

Rest, warm but not hot, food, peace, beauty and sleep
Lots of sleep
Rest until I'm bored with rest
But not just lazy rest

Horses to ride, a gym to work out, books to read, chess to play,
Ping-pong, badminton, even squash
Food, glorious food
How self-centred I am
Christmas is the time for giving and thinking of others

Well, I am entitled to be tired,
When you're tired you're tired
Even a horse needs rest
It doesn't mean I am not thinking of others,

I am fortunate, I have so much to be thankful for
So many others need rest more than I
Do I feel guilty – it sounds like it
But take care of yourself before you can care for others
Perhaps

Cow'rin, Tim'rous Meee!!

A secret stowaway in her car
"Confettied" Kleenex and tiny black specs
Gave him away
Fear gripped her now
In the realization that
This intruder was a MOUSE

Should it show itself
Panic could cause a crash
With socks pulled high over trouser legs
She prayed this passenger would stay stowed away
Azlan, the cat, would be her man
Several hours of being on duty
Azlan had no mouse to show

Another drive of terror
Work had to be attended
Mousetraps had to be bought
This mouse was smart
Bait taken but he stayed "untrapped"

Another day of nightmarish drives to town
A colleague suggested
Sticky paper traps
A stop at Home Hardware after work
A compassionate salesman
Suggested a more humane device
$20 later she left the store with a trap like cage
The mouse could enter but not leave
"Just lift the lid and relocate," he said

Next morning looking back at her from the cage
Were two bright black eyes and
A twitching tiny black nose
The monstrous mouse she had imagined
Was oh! so cute

She felt a glow of satisfaction
That she had spared this little creature
The words of Robbie Burns' poem "To a Mouse"
Scurried through her thoughts

Lucky her son Alexis was home
Because timid as this little creature was
She was still cow'rin with imaginings
Afraid to open the cage
They drove down the road
Alexis set the little stowaway free
In open pastures

Pink Toe Nails

It was impossible
To reach a verdict
There were no clues
To say who or why or what

They knew where
Spewed up out of the depths
By the breakers on the tide
An ocean's mystery

The puzzling question
To be answered
Said the Carpenter,
"Who painted the Walrus' toe nails pink?"

Mum Loves the Song
'Time in a Bottle'

Whirling Hands

I know where the time goes
Always racing as if it's late for supper
Hands whirling like the air in a tornado
Hands desperately trying to clasp the other
When they do,
Mildly pulling apart just in case someone catches them
Like young lovers racing round the raspberry bushes

Pockets

My pocket holds my future
There are pages in my pocket
Pages that tell me what to do and when to do it

Pockets sell the clothes I buy
For I need pockets for pages
For pages in my pocket tell my future

What to do and when to do it
Who's number to call
When I relax

The Painted Veil

The canvas of our lives
When the paint keeps coming
Sometimes with calm delicate strokes
Others wild and irrational

There are times it would seem
As if someone had thrown
A whole can of coloured paint
On the stretched cloth
Later to be veiled in shades of grey and black

A Rock

How many rocks to buy a baby
How many pounds in a stone
Daddy's gone a hunting with a sling shot
Baby swings in a glass house

It sits alone
Out of place
Solid – bold
Dull coated
Polished it would shine
Reflecting worlds passage
Inspiring future form

No High Stakes

There were no high stakes to attract the crowd
At least, none that were evident
You had to be smart to play this hand
It meant holding back,

Keeping things tight and close
Just until that perfect moment
Letting everything fly at once

Running forward, with head held high
Catching the shot, unwavering, standing firm
Only you knowing you won

Remembrance

Silent procession leads to the cenotaph
Cenotaph halts their step
Blood red poppies flowing at its feet
Trumpet echoes through cold autumn air
Remembering those slain

Churchyard cold and bleak
Chilled Autumn air
Silent procession leads to the cenotaph
Blood red poppies laid at its feet
Stand and remember

Barren Cliff

Each view of life is different,
Never the same, as the light falls
Each view of life changes,
Just as the light falls on photographic moments
Never to return again

How the wind circles,
Gathering new strength,
Hauntingly challenging those who dare

Radiant in your golden plume
So little time to show
Soon you will fall
Broken under strange feet
To shine no more

Bad Timing

It was 2:30am by the clock at the side of the bed
The rain was falling fast and heavy
6:00am when the clock yelled "Time"
And the fast falling rain was still fast
Too fast to keep up with at this time of the day
But the day had to be dealt with,
No matter how far she ran behind

Through the darkness there was no glimmer of sunrise
Sky rise or rain stop
Just the thud of the heavy drops on the world outside
Why did it have to rain today of all days
There would be no joy in a hayride at farmer Bill's today
Would those who had planned to attend
From Echo Village and Westhaven
Have dampened spirits
Or would they welcome the warmth to stay inside
I was dampened as we decided to cancel the ride
All those glorious autumn sunshine days and we had to book today
After the sun the rain, after the rain the sun

Tumbling Brooks

A year of many a sunny day
What joy to find November days bathed in sunshine
Mornings mist opening to silver and golden rays
Raising my lowly spirits to take me through another day

Temperatures well below – crisp, cold and freezing,
And together with the sun
Transmits energy which hours before had been sapped
By too many hours of work and physical demand

I regret having to go inside to work on days like these
I want to photograph, walk in the fallen leaves,
Go to the ocean and make footprints in the sand
Make a bonfire, rake the leaves – find a friend

Days now seem so precious
How fast the time runs by like the tumbling brooks
Gathering rushing rivers on their way to the open space of sea

I want to grasp at the beauty of these days,
Hold it close, like the flowers gathered,
It seems as if these moments play a game of hide-and-seek
When found I want to feel their presence always

Light

She stared out into the darkness
Passed the columns and paving stones
Which reflect the light from the café
Her gaze took her across the square to the street lamp
Under which the storm blown raindrops
Sparkled in patterns of light
Reminding her of a glimpse into a kaleidoscope

Daylight

The heaviness of the mist
Bringing the sky down to envelop all,
That sunlight usually awakens,
Has weighed me down all day

Curtailing my usual enthusiasm
To go out to walk or ride my bike
Substituted by a nap close to the fire instead

December
In 23 days the first day of winter will be here
The shortest daylight day
From then on it is a gradual climb to spring

Out of Time

You're no longer there to make the flowers grow
Nothing to make the dew drops glisten
Silenced

Our not so Fearless Mother

Life & Time

The past weeks have been a stream
Stream of work and toil
Fear and tears
Loss and Pain
This stream is hurling into a river

Torrents building
Current pulling one under
Down and down
Yet the circles above are still silver
Silver circles pulling back up like a top to spin and spin

That's life and time
Time so precious but you cannot hold onto it
Slipping away trying to grasp the moments
As they seem to evade glassy clutches
Some things should be left to fade
Never to recall the sharpness of the image

To see the blade cuts deep
Deeper than the first time
And yet you still walk too close
It will break you again
Like the ice on the stream
Cracking on fragments of memory and happenings

Distancing further and further away
When the day will become night
Never to brighten again as the tide pulls you under
Stronger than you

To the bottom as you crawl
With heavy boots made from words poisoned
By the arrowhead dipped into torturing thoughts
And the poison spreads until the body lies still
With no reason to carry on

Desolate

That tree is going to fall!
Weight distribution cannot prevent it
Rings and rings and rings and rings
Denoting age like wrinkles

Everything gravitates to this
This down, falling time,
When limbs and body hit the earth
Too much noise – crashing, hitting, twirling,

Precious moments hacked away
Until nothing remains
Lost for ever
No mourners, no legacy, no sounds, no peace

Was it worth the struggle, the giving, the caring
No one to care for, no one to care
And the rain falls,
But washes nothing away

Do please wash it away
Make the surface clear again
At least let some glimmer make it through
Just enough to cling onto with worn bleeding fingers

Searching for a reason – a reason for anything at all
If there is anything, anyone, anywhere
Hold on, hold on,
That tree is going to fall!!!

The Seniors Ticket

You never admit your age
So why did you purchase a seniors ticket
Reserving it in your name
For pick up at the door

On a list for anyone to read – to take note
Remember your name
Would the list be destroyed
Or kept for posterity?

So many know you
Do they know the men in your life
Who you have hidden your age from?
Now the secret is out
They will look at you
With different eyes now

Perhaps I could go back
And pay an extra $2.00
Stating a mistake had been made
But would my name be erased
From that reservation list?
Was it written in red ink?

Can I somehow get into the front desk
And tear out that page?
Never again will I purchase a seniors ticket
Will not until I am content with me again

Down, Down, Down

Gate closed ahead
Quagmire all around
Suctioning heavy feet
Hard to tread, to lift
Move forward forcibly
It will pull you under
To the depths of despair

Pressure gives, you move forward
Climb the gate
On the far side you can run
Feel the breeze caress your skin
Ruffle your hair
Released tears fall like summer rain
Setting you free

Where am I

Continuing, day by day, knowing the emptiness, the pain,
The longing for real meaning, heart searching for depth
Mind deprived of stimulating conversation and union
How long can one accept drudgery?
Is this all one can or should expect after so many years of living?
The best years given to return no more

Did you never think you would become old?
Did you really believe you could live like this for always?
Everything has its toll. The cost now seems profound
You were too afraid to let go
Not for yourself but for those you lived for,
The ones you cared for more than yourself

Now they powerfully set their own course, motivated and confident
Cut free from tender, nurturing arms
Hey! Wait for me
Don't leave me in the abyss alone
I need to hold on
Take me with you... Called out in vain

This is the time when the detour sign appears
The time to travel ones own route
Somebody forgot to erect the signage
Forgot to pave my road
I flounder like a crab on its back
The emotions are overpowering

Mind and body twisted with distress and grief for the loss of myself
Where am I? Where can I go? Who can I cling to?
Will anyone ever be there for me?
Is there anything left to retrieve or revive this worn out relationship?
The scene is familiar. It is safe here
I know the routine, the same pattern of conversation

My life possessions and material comforts fence me in
Completeness needs more than these things offer
I need to be able to give love again
My body is heavy with pain
I can no longer handle the mental stress
Within this setting I will never find direction

It will be necessary to look only at today
For I have no answers for tomorrow
Take courage and step out into the darkness of the unknown
In the hope that through its fearfulness and solitude
There will be a glimmer of expectation and fulfillment

One More Day

The gentle sound of the incoming waves soothing her heart
Like a mother's lullaby
A canoe passes colourfully by
With two orange life jackets and two yellow paddles
She regretted her empty camera

It is hot here, even though it's 7:10pm
Port Alberni must be an inferno
She had experienced great love in this very place
Sadly she accepts those times have passed
Alone, no one needing her or desiring her company

She shares the beach with a couple of ladies in late 80's
Another lady 70ish with her little Jack Russell
Now herself, greying, aging, a lady alone
This special place no longer the awakening of young love

But the setting of age
All too clear to her today
Only memories
If only one more day
One more time

Disappear forever
One more magical moment
When one holds one's breath
Afraid of reality

Watch the Rain

It rains as if the world is crying
Tumbling
Swirling
Round and round as emotions gather like clouds
Heavy, full of negative happenings

But plod on
Like a child in yellow wellingtons,
Splashing through the puddles
Squishing and splashing
Churning up all the fear and hesitation

Lover's Parting

For some time the storage box had haunted a corner of the room
She had been aware of its presence yet rarely given a glance
She was not ready to pack away those special treasures the box would store
Treasures which were as fragile as a snowflake upon her hair
Comforting as the sun's warming touch on a summer's evening

She observed the intricacies of these moments
She had known they were not hers to keep, only to glimpse at
Yet she had imagined they would be eternally hers
She still needed to hold them close, treasuring their familiarity
The fear of the emptiness without them chilled her
She could not put them away. Not yet

The painful reality that they were not hers to keep tugged at her heart
Begging her to let go
Beautiful as they were they could not bring happiness
Sadly and deliberately she lovingly wrapped each treasure
Placing them tenderly into the storage box
Overcome by the knowledge she may never hold them again

A few still evaded the wrap as she tried to convince herself
That it would not be wrong to keep them
She needed to be strong – to pull away
At last the box was full
The lid was in place but not locked down
As she had feared the strong desire to take a last look overpowered her

Even with the knowledge of the pain it would cause
She slowly reached into the box retrieving a few of its riches
Letting the covering which protected them fall away
Once more running her fingers over their beauty
As she did so, overpowering obstacles crowded
Fading the intensity of their pleasure

To delay now would only destroy perfection
In tears she made an effort to accomplish her only option
Salted drops soaking the crumpled wrapping paper
From now on she would only hold the memory of them in her minds eye
As the trees hold on to the fading leaves of summer

The Written Word

The written words of hate are more deadly
Than the gun filled with lead

Beautiful words hold her love
The web that holds the fly

The Fire Box

When she awoke,
The light filtered through the frost
On the inside of the window panes
Stretching her arms,
Sighing with her yawn,

Her breath sparkled as it ventured across her body
Pulling the sheets tightly up to her chin
They sounded like cracking ice
Cold to her touch

It must have snowed she thought
For she sensed the sound of insulation
Across the room she could see no life in the fire box
It would take some time to warm her cabin this morning

She visualized the wood crackling
The heat it would shoot across the room like splinters
She shrank from the task as her bones rattled with cold

Frozen with Fear

It was fear that made the lonely girl drop her glass
She had turned quickly,
Caught the dark shadow of a man through the window
As their eyes met
He raised his arms out wide like an angry gorilla
His eyes flashed reflecting the light from the room

Who was he
No time to think
She was alone
Frozen with fear
Would he really break in through the glass?

Car Starting on a Cold Morning

There it goes again
That damn neighbours car
Churning,
Burning gears,
Hurting ears
Depleting our sleep
Spiting out guts
Murder his guts

Yearning for it to spark
Start,
Get moving
Leave us to sleep
Key turns,
Starter screams
A scheme to wake the neighbours
Every morning

20th March, 2003

We knew he would
It was only a matter of when
Even if all the sand in Iraq had been rifled through a sieve,
Finding nothing,
The Blarney Bush Company would have been sure
Saddam had painted all his missiles of mass destruction,
With invisible ink
Only to have been washed off by the first rainstorm,
Exposing their power!
So they would have to make war before the rain came
Yes, the Iraqis need to be free of the tyrant Saddam,
But there was a different way
UN Sanctions and weapons inspections seemed to have been working,
US Veterans of the Gulf War
1000's of them have joined together to condemn the war

Where were you when the war broke out? How did you feel?
I was at the gym. The usual loud rock was switched off
The soundless TV's developed sound
And not a soul spoke for quite some time
I felt like crying as I envisioned the fear and helplessness
Of millions of ordinary citizens
Who call this weapon testing field home

We are so far away – life carries on
The alarm clock woke me as it always so obediently does
Regular routine, breakfast, work, mailed a birthday gift to my son,
Home, nap, dinner, writers group
But there is a difference
The radio is a constant report, analyzing,
What if's, was, how – first casualties – chopper crashed
An accident, not shot down – Sixteen British and US soldiers dead
Dead while the sand blows, the oil burns,
The bombs fall and people tremble

Peace
They say we have had peace for the past 57 years, but have we?
We may have in our own country
But real world peace
I don't think so

Peace is crumbling, decaying like a rotten orange in this world,
Greedy for fame and gain and self
Surely there must be something else they could do, like write
A world wide writing group

Funny Legs Day

It was the one with funny legs that caused a stir
Distinct for their wavering curve
All he could think of were the legs

He saw them while he waited for sleep to come
He imagined them in his dreams
They were legs never to be forgotten

Legs that stimulated his nerves,
Laid him bear and vulnerable
The hairy thick and black legs of the giant tarantula
Long legs which were huddled next to him when he woke

Cracks

He lay on his back looking up at the ceiling
Fear gripping him, tying his muscles into safety knots
He pulled his spine downwards into the wooden boards
Attempting to escape, squeeze himself out if only he could

There they were again, peering at him through the cracks,
Jeering, pushing the blackness of the cracks further apart
Opening up in order to reach down to him – poking at him,
They would tear him, if they made the cracks wider

They are coming, they are getting closer,
Sweat poured off his trembling body
He had to get away, the floor creaked beneath his pressure
If only he could get up and run,

If only his legs could allow him to rise
But they had been immobile since the accident
Besides, there were no windows, no doors, there was no way out,
Only through the cracks in the floor boards
The dark cracks where they take him

Only into blackness
With these creatures clinging to him like silly putty
Cold shiny, black, so black, falling,
Falling to the bottomless depth of the crack,
Chased by the cracks on the ceiling

Emperor for a Day

He had often judged
Resented the Emperor's power
Weary of his conceitedness
Fearful of his anger
If only he could change places,
Just for a day
Abuse him the same way he abused his people
Maybe then, and only then,
His stony heart might soften
Realize he had power in a different way

Much Ado About Nothing

Much are the struggles in a day
Ado with each failed attempt
About to withdraw, unable to ask for help
Nothing saps the spirit more than the loss of self

Looking-Glass

Shoes in the fridge
Card mailed without a message,
She wants to scream but someone might hear,
Turn away, remember her madness

There are places for people like her,
Where nobody waits to listen,
Where everyone knows what is best
A place lost within herself

Parallel

He had never travelled this way before
Filled with uncertainty
He continued to make his way
Darkness was falling fast
He would never reach her in time
Through the shadows
Moon beams danced in a clearing
Branches casting shadows
Creating a strobe light show
Images far from Earthly

He stopped
Afraid to go further
His eyes followed their movements
As they rose into the blackness
Leaving a fiery trail parallel to the moons beam

Resentful

The car stopped at the top of the driveway
Unable to enter due to a neighbour
Trailer blocking half of the entrance
It was March yet the discarded Christmas tree
Was still sitting on a soggy cardboard box
Half way down the driveway

A little further, a pile of raked fall leaves
Blocked part of the trail which led down to the home
Before the steps an old rusty metal frame
Supported overgrown grape vines
Causing him to duck almost double to make his descent
At the side of the house wall were empty canisters
Black and brown
On a dark night, could cause a fall

The front entrance door fitted badly
Allowing the damp winter chill to enter inside
Dirty, unkept carpet lay at his feet
While all around were papers, boxes, bags, shoes, packages, laundry
Not an invitation to stay long
The woman who came to the door looked clean and well kept
He could not believe this space belonged to her
As they went into other areas

Neighbours

Neighbours, do we have neighbours?
Wars are started for less
I sin every time I come home
My thoughts could launch a missile
Hopefully it would blast the neighbours to far away places
No detailed names are unintended to protect the innocent

Temporary Peace

The window opening onto the light
Channeling vision to the lakes view
A wooden dock
A row boat
Framed by the all encompassing mist

A backdrop to feelings
Cushioning heavy thoughts which are drawn out into the light
Eyes weightless as they float over the beauty
Forgetting the imbalance of unknown decisions
Temporary peace to the turmoil raging on the inside

All She Could Do!

She wanted to scream
To run, disappear
Yet all she could do was stand and stare
As crystal-clear glass balls tumbled from the display
Splintering into hundreds of pieces

As they reached the store floor
Each tinkle of glass an explosion in her ears
Crunched under the feet of passers by
Rushing to avoid the chaos
Ignoring her plight

She was alone now
But the tribune would be crowded
The consequences life shattering
If only she could run

Sometimes I forget

I had a good idea yesterday
But I can't remember what it was
I know it was fun
At least I think it would have been fun
For the thought of what I've forgotten feels warm and cheery

Whoever invented forgetting
Should have known it would cause such distress
For a thought that the mind thinks
Should be a thought to think forever
To think I've forgotten the thought which yesterday was so distinct
Is enough to stop me from ever thinking a thought again
For fear of the loss of a good idea

Crushed

She had noticed his bright green hat the first day she met him
He wore it with dignity and distinction
A hat to be desired
It fit her well
Though the lining was coarse
Her subconscious had softened the weave

Cruelly his image towered above her now
Taunting her dignity with eyes of steel
Standing on the bridge in the faded green hat
The lining poking through jagged seams

She reeled, stepped on and crushed
Like a discarded tin can
Waiting for the tide to carry her away
To depths where not even God could find her

Finishing Touches

Hands touch
Eyes electrify emotions
With energy
Igniting deepest passion
Two bodies becoming one
Creating two, three or more

Time passes, distances
Those who loved
 Strangers now
Destroying sanity with
War torn words

The Court Room door opens
The weight of Justice
Tips the scale of tension
One with Power to Judge
Makes the Finishing Touches

Mum has so much Love

Carnation

Carnation, a bright yellow carnation
Strong and firm
Resilient to the lack of moisture
Which makes them outstanding keepers
Sat in a single stem vase

The reward for a full primped hair buzz
This single bloom complimented the shinny head
Which its person had so gallantly stepped forward
To disrobe of its crowning glory
Glory of an unselfish act

"I saved it for you, I knew you were coming today"
"Take it with you"
A beautiful yellow carnation sits on my table
As a tribute to those I love who have battled with the horror of cancer
Think of one of the most wonderful people to run on this Earth
Terry Fox

Jubilant Spring

A face radiant as sunshine
Joy springing forth
Gentle as the fountains spray
He bubbles forth
Matching a mountain spring
Eager to bring life
Spirit awakening hearts
His energy contagious

Ordinary Heroes

He faces each day in pain
Struggles to get stiff joints mobile
To dress – shave – eat
Will he be able to eat – Get down to the Doctor
Will anyone be there to help – answer his call

Today he has a date to sing karaoke
Pills sloshed down with water
Extra pills to keep him moving
Makes it
Sings with his friends
Has fun

But like all outings this one ends the same
The trip back to the four walls he calls home
A place his illness has trapped him into
There is no escape

He struggles to get out of the car seat
Puts each stiff leg and foot in front of the other
Like a rusty tin soldier
He enters
And returns to his lot
This parting grieves us both
I admire and love my endearing hero

Aphrodite

Aphrodite
The goddess of love
Spoke to me this morning
Beautiful morning
Filled with light

Love reflected from the old lady's eyes
Radiant as the morning light
She held a disposable camera in her hand
Please, take my picture with the Bougainvillea
For my son

In a mother's heart
Her son brings warmth
I understand her love
My heart is full to overflowing
Now visiting close to my son

Afrodite was her name
She was taking love to her son
Soon I will be leaving love behind
With my son

Thursday Meeting

Everyone gathered in the conference room as requested
Everyone working that day was there,
Everyone *had* to attend,
As we looked at each quiet face,
Questioning the reason for being here
It must be for some real important reason
What had someone done
Are we all getting pink slips,
Downsizing

The spokesperson entered
First words
"There is no easy way to say this"
The words which followed were spoken
But for some reason the mind would not interpret much

Dead
Who was dead
What name
No it can't be
Not him
He was so young,
Early 30's
So caring,
Loved his job

Was gentle and kind
His face remembered
His gentle voice, his warm smile
This can't be true
Tears falling,
Streaming
Sobs and Kleenex being pulled from their boxes broke the silence
What can we say
He was here, and now?

How precious is each day
We must remember to live each to its fullest
Don't waste life on things not worthwhile,
Share,
Be part of,
Go along,
Sing along,
Dance,
Love,
Share,
Reach out,
Speak up

After what seemed an age the group dispersed
Back to their tasks
But only in body
I can see his face,
Sense his presence
Return his smile
You are here with me now
Find peace my friend
I will miss you

Rustling Words

Words typeset on white papers
Four separate bundles fastened with bands
The aged shrunken lady dressed in ethnic black
Had important words wrapped in these pages
Anxious to spread her news

There are four waiting for confession
In the quiet of the outer sanctuary
The pages are extracted
The Greek lady tries to balance and sort
The white sheets on her knee

Often they fall
In the silence the sound of rustling words fills our ears
The pages in order,
Excitedly handed out

In contentment,
The dear soul noisily returns the treasured script to her purse
I fold her mysterious words and place them in my purse
To await interpretation by my son
When the words will rustle again

Conflict or Chocolate

Everyone loves chocolate
And your favourite is the dark chocolate
Not milk
Dark chocolate with coffee cream inside

You can buy them for diabetics you know
Can't even tell the difference between fake diabetic and the real thing
So surely you can write about chocolate
Oh, yes, and it is good for the heart they say

Hearts owned with chocolate
Chocolate owned hearts
Chocolates that win the heart
Chocolates that say I love you
And I do, but you don't

But there were good times, the best,
And like all love stories it seems, the lovers part
Because something happens to that love
The love that held you so close

The love that was so hot it melted the chocolate
Rivers of chocolate falling away like melted wax from the candle
The heart laid bare,
Your love drowned and I could not revive you

Shrink, Grow, Erupt

The heart stops and starts
Changes rhythm
Beats fast and slow
Blood flows
Pulling life through the body

I think of the body
As I look at the word "Aloha"
A word that flows from the heart
Sincere warm Hawaiian greeting
A word of love, tenderness, patience,

I can't remember the exact order
But I learned about this "Aloha" today
And the warmth of the people who use it
Armchair Travel today with the residents
I work with in the seniors home

Sporting lays, flowers in their hair
And their delight in freshly made Hawaiian Sunday's
With banana, pineapple, coconut ice-cream
Fudge and chocolate
Very rich and decadent

Did you know that the landmass of Hawaii
Increases each year due to the volcanic eruptions?
I never thought about that until today
I have erupted many times
But my size does not increase no matter how much I pray

In fact, I am getting smaller by the month
Bet there are some who would like to change with me
If I thought erupting more often would help I would do so,
But there is little to erupt about
As my patience grows over the years

I often erupt with happiness
The joy of living
The excitement of something learned
The success of my boys
A horse ride with my granddaughter

But there is a different kind of eruption
Free and wild, throwing everything miles high
Screaming to drown out the wind and the roar of the waves
Crashing down and crushing all beneath you
Something has quieted within me
Can't erupt when you see the tenderness of life

The Way He Looked that Night

The car sped along
Carrying her closer to the agreed spot
Where he would be waiting
There was no doubt that he would be there
As always

Tonight was the eve of New Year
She had called because she needed to be with him
Could not think of being alone
His voice confirmed his own loneliness and eagerness
So he would be there

The night was dark
The headlights clearly illuminating his stature
As he stepped out of the shadows of the building
From curls to sole of shoe, arousing her desire
Etching feelings that would never let her forget
The way they were together
And the way he looked that night

Old Hands

"Old hands like mine..." he said
She had never thought of him as old
She had considered him to be
Warm, sensual, caring
A devoted husband

Age had never entered into her description of him
Old hands she had never seen
He was friendly Chester
Who gave her a warm feeling of home
Chester in Cheshire – England

If Only We were Free

Quietness and comfort
Knowing that we are loved
The stress of the day put away
Wrapped in clasped arms
The centre of a star that makes it into the day
If only we could be free without life's tangles
To drown in pleasures we have only imagined in our waking sleep

Loves Graffiti

He loves me, he loves me not
She loves me, she loves me not
Is it she who loved him or is it he who loved her?
The words unspoken on the sea-saw of emotions

She had given him a share of her soul
Risked so much,
Laid her heart down by his side
Yet, so easily he had rolled over her and extinguished the flame

Tears washed away all the smouldering embers chilling her flesh
Was the cut really that deep
Or had the wound connected with previous hurts
Opening a torrent of confusion, humiliation and rejection

She was left swirling to find her worth
Gathering control with strength of will to dam the pain
Until all the tender roots could build a new foundation
Had he loved her? Had she loved him?

What is love? Is it like time itself
A heartbeat passing by never to return
Or is it the hand of loves graffiti
Painting a tangled script of broken dreams

God's Child

The five year old Theophan
Held my gaze
Filled my soul with love
The presence of God's spirit
A gift given by divine power

On his head he wore a skoufa
From the Jordonville Monastery
Wore a black monks habit
A large wooden cross around his neck
His love for God's church and His servants,
Shone in his eyes, caught his step as he walked

His innocence and tenderness warmed my spirit
Put meaning into why I was here
At St. Anthony's monastery in the Arizona desert
Theophan, a pure heart on earth
Affecting me more than all the fine churches
More strongly than the priests and their rituals
He opened my locked soul
Shone the light of Jesus into my chilled heart
Renewed my faith

He reached out to those around him
His genuine love emanating from their faces
Two nuns from Greece glowed with happiness
As they greeted him during Vespers
I saw him take his mother's hand
Kiss it gently then laid his head against her
Such love, such peace

In his five short years Theophan had undergone seven operations
Suffered from multiple seizures
Spent weeks in hospitals
He had a major seizure today
His mother thought she was going to loose him

We all prayed for his recovery
His father carried him to the church
I put my arm around the tiny body
He felt so stiff
My son lent his own cross which had come from Jerusalem
Acknowledging Yorgo's thoughtfulness

I too offered Theophan my own hand carved cross
Given to me by Father Ephraim at my baptism
A cross hand-carved by him
While Abbot at a monastery on Mount Athos
Two hours later Theophan's angelic voice
Was singing hymns in the garden
No signs of harm

A monk said "Theophan gives blessings"
Cupping my hands before him
He made the sign of the cross
Laid his hand on mine
I kissed his precious tiny hand
Bless you Theophan, God's child

The Warmth of His Smile

Eighty-nine years – that's a lot of years
A lifetime – eighty-nine years
He had spent the past fifteen or so in the facility
Where he took his last breath
On Sunday 18th October 2004
Died peacefully in his bed
Peace after many a year had worn away the rough edges
So rough that most shied away from him
Forgetting at times he had feelings somewhere deep inside
That he had a heart, was human
A need to be treated with dignity – the basic of human needs
She had known him for almost six of these years
Had seen his pain

She had searched for the simple pleasure which brought him joy
Causing his face to beam like the sun
The weekly bus ride, the chocolate coated doughnut at Harbour Quay
The activity games he became part of
Assisting him to rise from his chair in the dining-room
His cup of juice and cookie
And in these latter months his night-time chocolate pudding
Today she stood by his coffin, placed three yellow carnations by its side
Spoke of him to those who had gathered
For the last stage of his journey
Spoke to the three mourners sitting before her
Only four to say Goodbye, but sad as this seemed,
In her heart the chapel was full because she was able to sand the edges
To recall his beaming smile
To travel with him
On the way to his final resting place at the Greenwood Cemetery
The sun warmed the small group
The birds sang – there was peace
A place to visit once in a while
To whisper his name and recall the warmth of his smile

True Caregiver

Corey...
Words spoken – not hearing
Denying their meaning
Questions – How? Why?

You left us
No chance to say goodbye
If only you had known
How much you are loved
By those you cared for
And those with whom you worked

Did we tell you?
We appreciated your thoughtful, loving ways
A true Caregiver to us all

I can see your face
I return your smile
Walking to ease the pain
I stoop to pick Snowdrops
Small, fragile, strong
Unafraid to greet the winter's icy cold
I think of you
Tall, strong, young, gentle
Quietly bringing comfort in difficult times

Snowdrops have new meaning
If not of Spring
Of hope eternal

We reflect
How precious each day

Find peace dear Corey
We will miss you

A Story for Another Day

She had never experienced the act of love
Why she had never experienced a man's touch
It was difficult to fathom
She was caring, attractive and open
Falling in love with a boy many decades her junior

He asked her to join him on a walk down to the cove
With the rock studded beach,
Jagged mounds creating secluded spaces
Softened by milky sand, washed high by the tides

They had meandered among these sculptures
Then stood, at first looking at the waters
Taking on the colour of the setting day
Then turning into each other their eyes met

She lifted her head and removed her horn rimmed glasses
He could feel the velvety dark eyes taking control of his own
Her body drew his close to hers with a power of its own
He reached out and took away the clip from her hair
And felt its softness as the tumbling beauty touched his chest

He could never have imagined such energy would have filled his day
Energy that could not be stopped
A meeting that would not end
But would lead to a story for another day

Two Souls Entangled

Met on the bridge
Caught in a swirl of warm autumn air
They danced with the breeze
Journeyed along the banks of the stream
Keeping rhythm with its soothing flow
Skipping across the ripples
As the sun threw glittering diamonds on the soft green water

They settled for a while on the banks beneath the shade of a tall maple
Colourful leaves almost kissing the pool of sparkling silver
Flowing water played a refreshing rhapsody
Interrupted by the splash of the dogs retrieving branches
What peace enfolded their spirits
Transfixed for a moment in time
Two souls gliding along like a paper boat with the current
Holding each other close so as not to let go of such tender beauty

Mum Always Loved our Family

His Gentle Spirit

The dessert lay beneath her
As she flew like an angel across Arizona
Yorgo did not know she was so close to him

She knew, the tears clouding her eyes
How she missed her son
His gentle spirit
The closeness they had shared

Now looking down from the blue
She saw him in spirit
Look up my child, I'm here, I'm here

Luggage

Time to part – how fast the time has flown
So much I had wished to discuss with him,
Now put on hold till the next time – hopefully soon
We hugged, kissed "I love you," "Be Safe"
Mom stood by the ticket office watching
Watching like a security guard,
To make sure the valuable packages make it onto the carts,
To be driven onto the 5:10pm ferry
By the time they were loaded,
The very last of the baggage,
He would be taking his seat on the ferry

It was a warm evening,
Golden sun making its way slowly on the horizon
She decided to take the coast road to Rutherford Mall
It was quiet – no traffic – no lights
The ocean seductively glistening
As she approached Pipers Lagoon,
She could not resist turning in
And making her way to the park
The salty air and beauty of the lagoon
With the ocean beyond
Calmed her spirit,
Reclaimed peace after that "beat the clock" drive
To catch the 5:10 which today decided to stay until 5:20

She took the camera from her briefcase
Intent on taking a picture of the ocean
For the next project of her Memory Plus programme
There it was, the BC Ferry carrying her son away from her
Back to his life on the mainland
She stood alone with her treasured memories of their times together
Joy filled her heart that he would spend his days off with her
The few days they share together each year now cherished

My Three Boys

I have just realized how very different each of my boys are
Just come to terms with the fact
That they are all three living their own lives the way they want to,
And they are happy where they are
And with the people with whom they live

It is I who is holding on to what we used to share
Longing for life to continue with them
As my companions to enjoy life with
But that would not be good for them
They need the freedom to carve their own path through life,
To enjoy it to the full with their own chosen partners

For me I will have to accept the short times we will spend together
When I feel complete again
And store the memories as the incredible gifts they are
Like buried treasures in the depths of my heart and mind,
Reliving them at any moment I choose
To bring them forward to the present,

Today dream in memories
Now I know what my Grandmother
And the seniors with whom I work
Do when they just sit looking at the garden,
They fill the space with the image of people they love
And hold them close

The Meeting Place

She waits anxious
Praying that nothing prevents their rendezvous
Tucked away in a brown paper bag
Are all the special treats she could find
For today, Sunday, they may eat together
A picnic
By the black cross with coloured lights

Twelve noon
Four minutes to go
Has he woken
Will he come
Does he need a blessing to meet his mother
Will it be granted
Don't disappoint your mother Yorgo

Two minutes to go now
She waits like a young girl
Wondering if her loved one will come
Sunday lunch with the Monks is special
She only hopes he desires this special time with her
At the agreed meeting place

It is twelve noon
Could that be his voice in the distance?
Someone speaks his name
Still she waits
Her heart leaps
He is here

Joyful Morn

The sun was just rising
As she and her son stepped lightly through the dessert
Dodging the cactus and spiky thorns
They were on their way to check out the Prophet Eliza church,
On first mountain

The air was refreshingly cool
After the heat of the church and trapeza
The light was pure and golden
Clothing God's creation in radiant beauty
Her heart was singing again
In the company of her beloved son
Her friend sharing mutual joy

Longing for this sun to never set
Grasping treasured moments
Knowing the joyful morn will fade away
Leaving memories to hold
When the tears of parting fall

Sunbeam

What's in a name?
Nikko is his name
Nikko, Japanese word for sunbeam
A ray of sunshine
To bring sparkle to each day
Warmth to his mother's soul
A wondrous gift from above
Fulfilling prayer
Sunlight
Sundrenched
Son Blessed

Footprints

Paris is old now,
Old for a dog that is almost sixteen
A legend the neighbours say
He makes his calls each morning
Around his regular route
His long, elegant legs carry
His thin aging, degenerating body

Should he not be seen for a day or two
Phone calls are received to ask if he is ok
Special treats are purchased for him by many
One day he was found sleeping in Vivian's bed
In her home across the road

Our door has deep grooves
From door-handle to step
Stripped down to the bare wood
The garden is flattened by his passing
The daily paper stamped by his paws
As the days with us are numbered
I accept his footprints like treasures

The First Time a Piece of Art Moved Me!

Viewing many great pieces of art
Galleries in London, exhibiting Bridget Riley, Andy Warhol,
The greats of the 60's
Constables
Stubs, Monet,
Yoko Ono's "365 bottoms" and "The Wrapping Up Event"
Wild, weird, extreme, daring to be different – very different
The ornate frescoes in St Mark's Cathedral in Venice
Standing in the same room as the Mona Lisa in the Louvre
Staring into the intensity of her penetrating eyes
Looking up at the naked tree on a dark rainy night, lit by street lamps
Following the illuminated concentric circles, God's creation

Yet nothing can compare with the excitement and joy
Bubbling forth from my three year old son, Nikko,
As he saw the results of his first masterpiece
Paint on my half of the page, fold it over,
Press it down, open it up,
The image is duplicated onto the opposite side of the page
Mirrored
Just to witness the joy of his creation
Touched deep emotions of the joy of his creation through me

Solo Flight

Soaring Solo
Silver Wings compose a rhapsody of blue
Free spirit surfs cumulus clusters
On a flight path to silver linings
In the vaults of heaven

For Yorgo Roscoe Roumanis
New pilot – 19 August , 2003

Alexandros

Alexander, Alexis, Alexi
Strong and noble
Rich cultural heritage

Forth son on the family tree
Welcomed home by Yorgo's precious security blanket
Nikko's caring brotherly love
Octopus hiding in a lost rock
Mom's kisses rubbed into his bones
Perhaps the foundation of interest in Paleontology
And the world of science
Greek ants treated to a bus ride in the dust
Guided by a born teacher, patient and kind
A dramatist
Mom envisioned
A singer a dancer
Tiny black ballet shoes
Retired from tiny feet
Worn only times three
Traded for soccer/wrestling boots
Exchanged only for larger size
Champion wrestler
Reaching for the international stage

Dynamic Star

Up on a mountain high
An outstanding performance
On SFU's amphitheater
A champion of degree
Gruelling discipline
His mother's eyes
Fill with pools of salted water
Gazing on her dynamic star

My Book of Life

You arrived
A new page in my book of life
Your story to unfold
Paragraphs followed
Inscribing wonder in my heart
Greater than I had ever imagined
Enriching chapter by chapter

Your achievements my life giving force
Now, in later years
Your mother turns back the pages
Reading the story in moments of solitude
Embracing each imprint
The narrative will continue
With hope and great expectation
Filling the pages until the book of my life is complete

Thank you Alexandros
Love you for always
Mom. 23 March, 2010

Desert Spring

Under the desert spring sky
Her heart is reunited with his gentle spirit
A spirit flowing as spring water
From the son she loves

Six hours of visiting time
Spread over nine days
At St Anthony's Monastery
Six hours bringing life
To the wilderness

Her heart blossomed
Like spring cactus flowers
In their radiant glory
She sang a song of resurrection
Alive in the spirit of her son's closeness

Today, the 9th day
The day to say goodbye
The dessert will be watered with her tears
Tears falling to the rocky ground
As blossoms fall from cacti
When their time for radiance is over
Under the desert spring sky

What do You Mean
Mum had a Youth?

Grandma's Cellar

The kitchen was lit only by the flames from the coal fire in the grate
Oh, yes, the home did have electricity
But my Grandmother refused to turn the lights on
She would sit in her chair by the hearth and look into the fires glow
Just sitting and to my young years – doing nothing

But now I'm grown
I know she was very busy reliving her life in her memories
A young husband taken from her through a heart attack
Her struggle to keep the farm and bring up her two sons

Taking on the job of Village Post Mistress to help with the finances
She converted one of the living-rooms
This is a child's delight
A candy store of your own

Before taking off for a ride on my horse
I would fill my pockets with my favourites
There were some candies in the Quality Street tin
That no customer ever got to have in the quarter pound
Because I picked them out every time a new tin was opened
I wondered if anyone ever realized there was something missing
When they bought from my Grandma's Post Office

Back to my Grandmothers, and the fire
When I came in from a winters ride, frozen, feet like blocks of ice,
She would sit me down,
Lower the metal door which contained the ashes
And tell me to put my stocking feet on it
This was so wonderfully warming
But she was the culprit in my getting chilblains

She would make tea and either cook some potato cakes
Or give me a huge slice of warm fresh bread smothered in butter
We would gaze into the fire together
Searching for images amongst the coals

Grandma's house always had a damp musty smell to it
The cellar was off the kitchen and there was a well down there
During the war this cellar was the village's air raid shelter
Everyone apparently would come
I wonder what that must have been like
What they talked about,
How close they felt to each other

Years later, when I used to go down there
I remember the root potatoes stored there
And the odd frog
That had somehow got itself down there via the coal shoot
No trees left to burn in England
Long gone
Coal was the fuel of the day

The cellar was always cool and eerie,
Not a place to hang around in for too long
Maybe that was a plus
When all those bodies gathered there
To evade the torments of war
It would probably be hot and stuffy then
But we never discussed those days

The School Gardener

Glass eye
Look at my eye
It was a catapult
As I played with the boys at school
Beware

Jupiter

My horse
Liver Chestnut
Elegant, lively, strong
Oh Jupiter I remember
Our time

1960's

A time for change
Cancer hit hard and strong
Claimed her body after diagnosis
Mom died
Her last breath taken
With three daughters by her side

Father missing
Distanced from her
By many troubled years
That demon in the bottle
Took him away from us all
Loved with a child's heart
Hated Mr Hyde
Wished away

A Sun Speckled Trail

Chest pounding
Weighted down as the fog compresses the earth
Air crisp and fresh, the sun struggles to break into the day
Pools of blue through the mountains of grey
Win the tug of war as the sky turns electric blue

She longs for a steed to mount
That would carry her off down a sun speckled trail
Cantering through freshening dewdrops
Casting away the ties of tangled paths,
Which twisted her into knots like weeds in the curve of a creek

This had been her escape in her childhood
The way she survived her youth
Listen – can you hear the sound of hoofs on the gravel?
Feel the air fresh on your face until eyes water and stream
Forcing out unwanted thoughts

A Child's Scariest Seesaw

I go back now to the darkened room
A small child lying in my bed
Unable to sleep
Turning, twisting into painful knots
Listening and waiting for his return
Mr Hyde
The servant of the devil in the whisky bottle
What would that monster have him do tonight

Where was my mother
Was she sitting in the living room
With thoughts and feelings like my own
Did she want to run and hide, never to return?
I know she did
I heard her tell an Aunt that she only stayed because of me
Was I to blame for the torture she endured
Or did she really love my father and the daytime Dr Jekyll?

He was a gentle, kindly figure
Interesting and always willing to ride the horses with me
For miles and miles along well hoofed bridal paths
Besides rivers and canals
Caring for the animals on the farm
He was good in the daylight
Wether the sun was shining or not
But he never said he loved me
No one ever did say they loved me when I was young

There's the door now
It won't be long now before he gets started
How did it begin
I don't know, but it always did
The arguing and fighting
I put my head under the pillow in an effort not to hear
But maybe the pillow was not thick enough
Or maybe the young ears were acute

It went on for hours
And somehow
I don't remember how
Sleep came and it was morning
The house was quiet and another day of pretence started all over again
But I loved him, and I hated him
And for a young child this was a painful frightening seesaw to ride

Whoosh

How many times had she heard that sound
Whoosh, whoosh, followed by explosive cracks and bangs
Each time it was heard the memory came flooding back,
Arousing feelings deeper than the first time
And far more painful

It had been forty years now,
Yet she still bore the scars, inside and out
There had been all the usual excitement and hype
Which all young children rise on
The evening was clear
Clothed in the chill of autumn

She held the hand of her elder brother
And they walked down the street to the community centre
While she stood there gazing at the huge bonfire
Her memory recalls that whoosh
A whoosh which was silenced as it tried to bury its cargo into her face

She saw the huge flash of light
Then felt the pain and the burning
She could still hear and feel her scream
She heard the worried voices of people around her
The sound of ambulance bells

Then there were the bandages
The many days in hospital in the darkness
The darkness which had been with her now for forty years
She had petitioned and rallied to abolish fireworks
Told her story, shown her scars
But none had heard her
As she heard the whoosh she prayed for the safety
Of all the little people out in the streets this Halloween

Wasn't it a Party!

Those were the days of my youth in the city of London, England
The regular parties, dancing, drinking,
Until the wee small hours of the morning
Great music, great friends, great dancing
This particular one I remember was at New Years
Probably about 5am, and myself being the most sober
At the wheel of the car
As the four of us drove back home across London

There they were, Police, flagging us down at their road block
My heart sank
Yet in those days they were not as keen as they are now
They were on the passenger side of the car
Which meant they could not catch a whiff of my direct breath
Ian wound down the window

Then Phil, an Irish girl who had plenty to say when she wasn't drunk,
Started to flirt with the Bobby
"Oh Officer, come in here an join me"
"How are you Officer," etc, etc,
I was just praying she would shut up
However, perhaps this helped as they were so taken up with Phil
That they hardly paid any attention to me
They wished us a happy New Year and sent us on our way

First Experience with Alcohol

It was Christmas day in England
With the heap of mail being delivered
By our faithful Postman
He came by bike
As in previous years
He was invited in to partake of a Christmas drink
My father would pour the biggest glass full of Scotch Whisky
And the Postman, whose name eludes me,
Would drink it down into his already well oiled body

When he took his leave,
We would all gather around the windows
To watch as he attempted to mount his bicycle
After several attempts we would watch,
Laughing ourselves silly as he weaved his way down the village road
Which fortunately in those days, was free of traffic

At that time, my first experience,
Alcohol seemed entertaining
But, sadly, in the years that followed
I was to find out that a devil lived in those bottles
Changing my father from a Jekyll to a Hyde

Dancing Hooves

The morning was mild and wild
Strong breeze
Black clouds
Bursting to throw down torrents of rain
Through branches
Then, as in the hymn,
After the rain, the sun
Sparkling in the puddles
So mild I took several residents for a spin in the garden
Air fresh, touched with a burst of spring
"Glad that I live and that the sky is blue"

In these moments I feel so alive
Never wanting to go back indoors
I want to jump on my horse again and take to the bridle paths of home
To gallop and feel the breeze on my face
Ruffling my hair
Hear the sound of the hooves on the soft earth
See the trees swaying,
The water rippling
Distancing any concerns far, far behind

The days are getting longer
No more is it dark at 5pm
The promise of spring is here as green shoots poke through
Soon the snowdrops and daffodils
Will be dancing in all their colourful splendour
Delicate, and hardy to the chill of the north winds
"Beside the lake, beneath the trees, fluttering and dancing in the breeze"
Not my words you say,
I admit they are not,
But such beauty catches the eye of us all

New Year

The eve of the Bards Memorial Day
His birthday
Our lad of fame
Robbie Burns
Time has not forgotten him
Better known now than he was in the 18th century
Celebrated
Recited
Piped and danced in dignified ceremony
Robbie
A man close to nature
And lover of the lassies

Bedtime stories for me as a very young girl
Younger than five
Were Robbie's poems read and explained by my father
My dad held Robbie in great esteem
My favourite memory is the story of Robbie
Sitting next to someone name dropping at a dinner party
Robbie tiring of hearing his pride turned to him and said,
"A louse, sir, is still a louse. Though it crawl on the locks of a queen"
This really left an impression in my young mind
As I envisioned a louse in the hair of our Queen Elizabeth of England
Wondering how with all those servants she had dirty hair!

Robbie, a farmer
Was close to nature,
Felt pity for the injustices rendered upon the wild creatures
As in *To a Louse* and *To a Mouse*
He always drew parallels with our human fate and challenges

Robbie is to be admired
Not having the money to be educated as those favoured by birth
Self-taught yet it was claimed he outshone Byron with all his privileges

The Satin Tapestry

It was actually the keepers who failed
The satin tapestry had been a family treasure
At Chatsworth House for years
Catalogued as a remarkable piece of workmanship and art
If only she had done the right thing
When those cuddly two stood innocently on the grand entrance steps
If only she had not invited them in
The kittens would never have chased those mice up and down the satin
Like ice skaters scratching their blades through a glassy surface
Finders will be punished for keeping

Influence

Forbidden to see my bestest friend anymore
"She's going to influence you" they said
"She's too old for you to be with"

We had fun
In the loft at Lord Whitley's farm
Taking turns pushing each other in the retired perambulators
Dusty and cobwebbed
Sacrilege to treat them with such disrespect
Would be a high priced antique find today

We had fun rowing boats when our bicycles took us to the lake
She wanted to attract the boys in the other boat
I didn't mind

We passed notes to each other in the choir stalls during the sermon
Something was funny
Until the choir master's eye caught us in his mirror
Placed strategically above the organ
Thunderously he banged on the wood panelling and scowled at us
We were drawn to the congregation's attention – plus my parents
"You can't see her anymore – she's a bad influence on you"

Bury Me Standing

Shake the corn ears
Sounds of muffled bells
Like a rush of frozen droplets – yet not frozen
Free, separate, rushing down the chute
Filling the corn bin
The sun's golden rain
Seeds, earthy, fresh
Shrouds my body – tightly woven
Bury's me standing

Grandma's Kitchen

In Grandma's kitchen every Sunday for tea
We had canned fruit swimming in Carnation milk
Cherries, plums, orange segments, pears,
And enhanced by the little can,
With its red label and white lettering
A can of Carnation milk takes me back to those days long ago,
Sitting on the open horsehair stuffed chaise longue
Cat on the floor hoping to get a taste

The old radio and the drawer underneath it,
Bulging with pieces of neatly wound lengths of string
Grandma kept all the string that she chanced upon
She had been through the war you see
And she kept many things
Which she felt may once more be impossible to come by
Should the country go to battle again

I can see her hair pulled tightly back in a bun,
She had a gentle face,
Not severe with such a hair style
And she wore her apron
The latch on the door which led to the outer kitchen
I can hear loose metal connecting
Connecting me back to the past

The Austrian Gypsy

Only a memory now
Facial features veiled by time
But the memory of his body lingers
Sunburned skin, weathered,
The smell of wood smoke on his clothes

Strong, arms supporting his guitar
Skilled fingers racing over the strings
The life, depth and wildness of his voice
As he moved close to her table
Looked into her eyes as he sang

He drew her desire for him as he implied he desired her
Come with me he whispered in her ear during the applause
D A N G E R signals rang in her head
Crisscrossed with the enchantment,
Of this earthy sensual gypsy

To step outside into the night in Austria
A country she had only known for a day
With this tempting stranger
She was young, only nineteen, yet not a fool
But her heart went with him for a while when he left
And his memory arouses excitement still

It's Time to Think

When the words won't come
She struggles to be understood
Trapped within her memory
Pictures of yesterday

Yesterday, when one day seemed as long as seven
Time to lie in the wheat field
Hear the breeze through golden ears
Like an ocean's swell
So much freedom

Age had not shown its challenges nor its furrows
There was years of time then
The end never contemplated
Yet today the mirror returns a different image
It's time to think said Alice

Homeward Bound

Strange, living here in Port Alberni for 29 years
The longest time I have lived anywhere
Yet deep, deep feelings of home seem to carry me across the miles
Back to my north England Village
Where I lived for only 17 years

Strange that living in Port Alberni I only just discovered a place here
Which transports my mind and soul
Unearthing deep rooted emotions of oneness with God's Earth
My secret place – McCoy Lake Road by Thompson's farm
Deep breaths of air filled with the smell of cattle, fresh cut hay
Sounds of chickens clucking, tractors harvesting
Small pony calling from the paddock
Blackberries ripe and sweet
Why did it take so long to discover
Such a place that takes me home
Hedges, trees, small country lane
When I stand with you
I am homeward bound

Retro Day

My 'Girlfriends Closet'
Search for yesteryears
Image of the sixty's

Wardrobe of the past
Dressing with style
Era reborn

Some play slots
Gamble high stakes
She buys clothes

Mom – The Dream

She was sitting on the ground at the station
Sitting with her legs stretched out in front,
Her back supported by the unpainted picket fence
As the sun warmed her face
Not many were waiting for the train,
When she first found herself sitting there

But by the time the sound of its whistle was heard,
There was quite a crowd
The smell of coal fire and steam filled her nostrils,
The power of its breaks filled her ears
Carriage doors flung open and passengers alighted
She had not been sure who she was waiting for,

But then she saw her
Felt her love and familiarity
Jumping to her feet, all the pain drained away
She was here, coming towards her, arms outstretched
She ran to her mother's open arms

As she closed them around her there was emptiness
No mother inside them,
The sun had gone, her body drained
Then tears fell and fell,
And she sobbed as the reality of a dream unfolded

The Fox Hunt

The hunt I am going to tell you about is very different from a deer or moose hunt you may be familiar with in Canada.

Imagine a crisp, frosty morning. A morning when you can see the breath of man and beast. The sun breaking through the mist awakening the countryside as the dewdrops sparkle like diamonds.

Horses hoofs clatter on the pavement. Horses calling to each other charged by the contagious excitement of the morning.

The main players of this days event, the hounds, banter back-and-forth like elementary school children at recess.

Imagine the scarlet red jackets of the Huntsmen. The shrill sound of the Hunt Master's horn as he and his Whipper-ins control the pack of hounds.

Hound is the official name for the dogs. Never let a huntsman hear you call his Fox Hounds, dogs. That is considered a crime.

Imagine the chatter of those riders who have come to join the huntsmen and hounds in the chase. They are dressed in formal hunting style – looking neat and well pressed, among whom you will find the few ladies who prefer still to ride side saddle. Instead of a tie, the hunting stock in worn around the neck. A wide white fabric, similar to a tie – yet tied differently.

The meeting place is the *village pub* – stiff brandy or whisky is handed around on silver trays by the pubs landlord. Hip flasks are filled for emergency!

The Master of the Hunt sounds his horn for the hunt to move out. The colourful group clatter down the road to the nearest wooded area to sniff out the scent of a fox.

While everyone else was sleeping, men had been busy filling in the entrances to the foxes den. There was no such thing as fairness in this sport. So the poor fox returning from his own evening hunt was unable to re-enter the safety of his lair. Should a fox find a way into his den, termed, *gone to ground* he is shown no mercy. Ferrets are put down the hole to drive him out of his hiding place. A ferret is a European albino polecat. Very vicious. As I said before, there is not fair play.

Farmers support the hunt as the fox often kills his animals. The farmers would maintain their hedges and fences without wire to enable the hunt to follow the hounds by jumping over fixed fences from field to field. This is not to say that there is no danger in jumping a fixed post and rail fence.

There is nothing like the excitement of the chase – galloping across fields and down country lanes, jumping fences. Eyes watering, ears tingling, in the cold winter air. Sometimes caught in falling snow. This is why I went hunting, for the chase. I never gave a thought to the main purpose for this barbaric ritual. The Dictionary definition of Barbaric is "Relating to, or characteristic of people that are not fully civilized."

Let me tell you why I use the term Barbaric.

When the fox is caught by the hounds, called *the kill*, this is what happens...

The Hounds have not been fed for a day hence their eagerness to tear the fox apart. The squeals, yelps and cries are chilling. The Master of the Hounds uses his horn and the Whipper-ins attempt to call off the hounds with cracks from their whips.

I made the mistake when very young of keeping up with the front of the field. Now the description of this Barbaric Ritual.

The first man on the scene receives the *mask* – the head of the fox which is cut off. A trophy for his wall.

The first woman on the scene receives the *brush*. The tail of the fox. How's that for gender discrimination. Why can't the women get a head?

The first children and youth on the scene receive a *pad*. The feet. These pads are dipped into the blood of the head then this blood is smeared onto the cheeks of the first four children/youth to arrive on the scene. The blood not to be washed off but allowed to wear off.

The body of the fox is thrown to the hounds to eat and fight over.

In conclusion I want you to know I am ashamed to say I went through this uncivilized ritual. It bothered me greatly and I decided at that time there was no such thing as civilized man. I kept well back in the field from then on and never again saw a kill... Things have changed now thanks to those who fight for the Prevention of Cruelty to Animals. Most hunts, which remain, now hunt by Drag. That is, a dead fox is dragged through the countryside leaving a trail for the hounds to follow.

Mum's Short & Sweet

still misty harbour
she sits thinking
eyes flooding like high tide

harbour fogged over
she loved and lost
silent ending

misty silent harbour
thoughts of love lost
boats on ice cold water

deep puddles
raindrop filled
reflections of blue skies

Flowers of spring
Catching the rain
In earthenware pots

quietly together
louder than words
no earthly reason to change

rock of ages
diamonds for ever
rock a bye-baby

Fields of melting snow
woolly lambs frolic
spring awakening

framed window
vision of centuries
perched on ghostly walls

windows in ruins
stately vision of centuries
on ghostly barren walls

stealing identity
alzheimer strips mind
loss and confusion

bird's song
quietened by stealth
feathers strewn

views of past and present
eerily withstanding time
ruined stones

SIR ARTHUR CONAN DOYLE

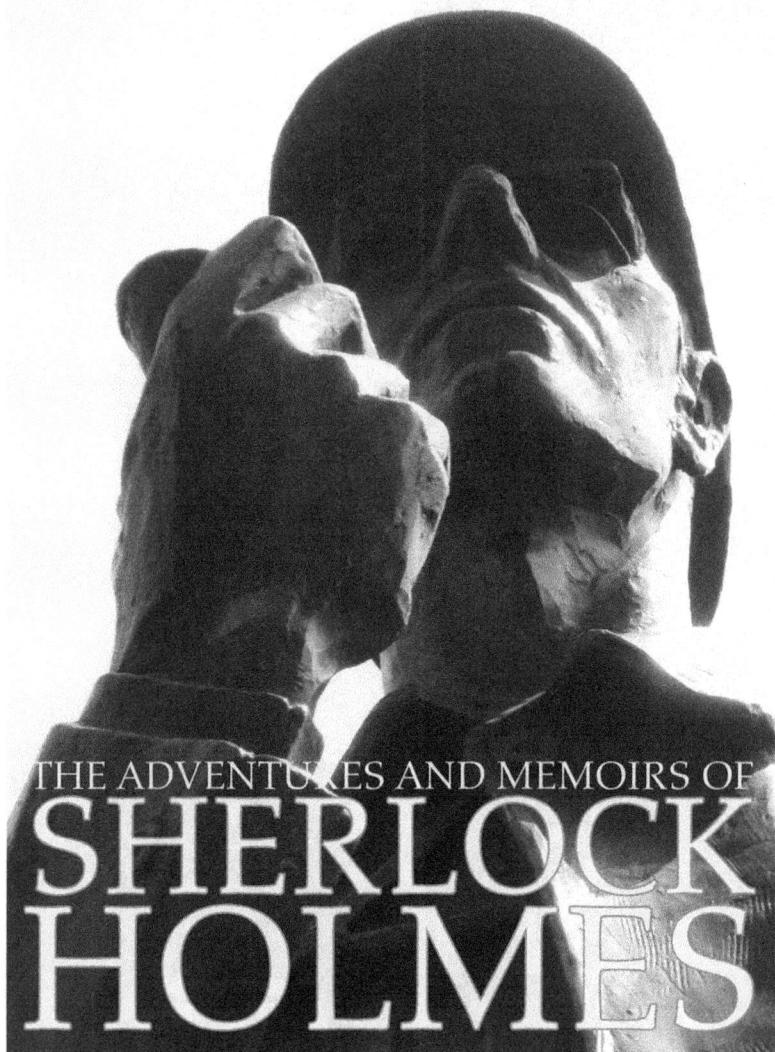

THE ADVENTURES AND MEMOIRS OF
SHERLOCK HOLMES

ISBN: 9781926606361

ILLUSTRATED

Available at

WWW.ENGAGEBOOKS.CA

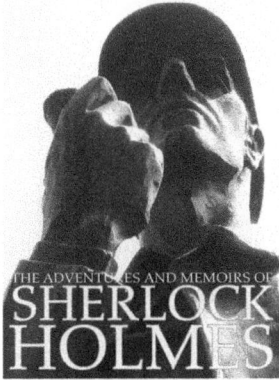

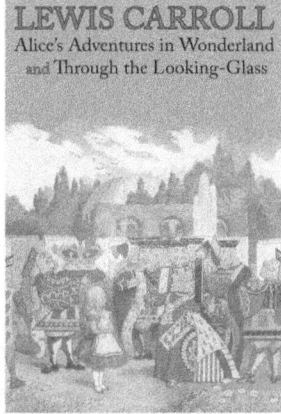

www.ingramcontent.com/pod-product-compliance
Lightning Source LLC
LaVergne TN
LVHW011328080426
835513LV00006B/247